Separation and Divorce: Helping Children Cope

The PACTS series: *Parent, Adolescent and Child Training Skills*

Separation and Divorce: Helping Children Cope

by
Martin Herbert

BPS BOOKS

THE BRITISH PSYCHOLOGICAL SOCIETY

First published in 1996 by BPS Books (The British Psychological Society), St Andrews House, 48 Princess Road East, Leicester LE1 7DR, UK.

A catalogue record for this book is available from the British Library. ISBN: 978-1-85433-190-8

Typeset by Ralph Footring, Derby.

Contents

Separation and divorce: helping children cope

Introduction

Aims

The aims of this guide are to provide the practitioner with:

➤ an understanding of the implications of separation and divorce for children;

➤ guidelines to help parents prepare children for the break-up of the parental relationship, and cope with the aftermath;

➤ some ways to help children express the powerful, painful emotions aroused by their parents' decision to separate.

Objectives

To fulfil these aims, the guide assists the practitioner to:

➤ assess the impact of divorce on children;

➤ plan interventions with grieving children;

➤ help parents communicate difficult issues to their children;

➤ think through with parents matters arising from single parenthood and reconstructed families, such as step-parenting;

➤ counsel divorced parents by means of a problem-solving, self-empowering course, outlined on pp. 24–30;

➤ explore the literature on divorce.

Note

For an increasing number of households, the impact of separation on children is the breakup of a parental (co-habiting) partnership, rather than of a marriage. This guide also applies to the difficulties and pain experienced by these children and their alienated parents.

Part I: All the King's horses and all the King's men

Consequences of divorce

Like Humpty Dumpty, many marriages have a great fall and cannot be put together again. In fact, so many marriages will falter or fail irreparably, that over one quarter of the babies born in the UK today are likely to experience parental separation before they reach school-leaving age. Divorce is a decree which affects *all* the members of a family, not only the marriage partners. It is the life event that receives the second highest stress rating out of forty-three potentially traumatic circumstances listed on the Holmes and Rahe Social Readjustment Scale (1967); and indeed it is one of the most common adverse life events experienced by children.

People tend to assume that children from broken homes are at a disadvantage in life, and will suffer inevitably from emotional or behavioural problems. Some children *do* suffer such intense emotional trauma when their parents divorce that they never fully recover from the detrimental effects; the psychological effects often persist into adult life, sometimes with a barely conscious level of awareness of what is wrong (see Wallerstein, 1991). Research findings indicate that individuals whose parents had divorced or separated were twice as likely as those from unbroken homes to have marriages which also ended in divorce or separation, thus perpetuating detrimental reactions from one generation to the next. Rutter and Madge (1976) have cited divorce as one of the factors that result in 'intergenerational cycles of disadvantage'. There is also some research evidence that childhood life events like divorce can influence parenting skills in later life. Of course, divorce *per se*, is not the only source of long-term problems – it is not surprising to find that many children are affected by the strains of acrimonious family life that *precede* separation and divorce (Cherlin *et al.*, 1991).

The alleviation of the consequences of divorce, and its precursors, for both parents and children, thus becomes especially urgent and necessary (see Cantor and Drake, 1983). Yet, while divorcing couples automatically seek legal guidance, relatively few seek professional help with their emotional problems. Lawyers cannot help with the painful emotions (anger, guilt, hurt, anxiety, despair) of adults who face the failure of a partnership, nor can they help those children whose parents are too preoccupied with themselves to be able to satisfy their needs. More often than not, children are neglected during a divorce and left in an emotional vacuum. However, the family is a social structure which continues to exist after it has been legally dissolved, and people who attempt to deal with the family as solitary individuals independent of each other, do the child no service. The child's well-being depends on his/her ability to maintain close emotional contact with *both* parents. A situation where the child is torn by a conflict of loyalty is a recipe for disaster. The child is likely to be fond of both his/her parents, however unreasonably they may have behaved towards each other.

The motto, ideally, might be, 'If we cannot make a success of our marriage let us at least make a success of our divorce … for the children's sake'.

The impact of divorce

Divorce is interpreted by many children and adolescents as a rejection or desertion of themselves. They do not, or cannot, comprehend all the adult implications of an unhappy marriage. On one hand, the assumption that divorce will have unfavourable consequences does not allow for the many children who overcome their grief and the disruption of their most intimate relationships and grow up to be normal, reasonably contented members of the community. If all divorces, all broken homes, led to serious psychological difficulties, society would indeed have an appalling problem on its hands.

On the other hand, the highest risk or likelihood of divorce (at present) occurs in the fourth year of marriage. In other words, it is very likely that it will be *young* children who are involved in the lead-up to, and aftermath of, a divorce. Separation – the event that really hits children – is likely to precede divorce by several years. And there is no doubt (as we know from many studies) that separation *is* deeply distressing to children. With the world falling apart for most of the adults who go through the trauma of separation, it is only too easy to overlook, downplay, or fail to support the distressed child. What happens to his/her feelings of desolation, anger, sorrow, shame or bewilderment? What happens to children is very much like the bereavement process that follows in the wake of that ultimate separation and loss, death. In some ways it is worse if there is endless hankering for reunions that cannot take place, or loyalty-dividing acrimony between the beloved parents.

You may have read that children hold themselves responsible for the break-up of their parents' marriage and feel very guilty about this. In fact, such reactions do not seem to be very widespread; much more common is anger towards the parents for separating. Children of all ages frequently express the wish that their parents be reunited, and they blame either, or both of them, for the split; most children do not want their parents to separate and they may feel that their father and mother have not taken *their* interests into account.

A marital separation may result in children reappraising their own relationships with their parents and, indeed, questioning the nature of all social relationships. For younger children in particular, there is the painful realization that not all social relationships last forever. If mum and dad can end their marriage, what *is* safe? Couldn't the same thing happen to their own relationship with mum or dad? Many childish reactions at such a time are expressions of the fear of being abandoned by one or both parents, and such fears are likely to be most acute if contact has been lost with a parent. If, however, relationships between parents and child can remain intact and supportive, these fears are usually short-lived.

The bonds of love

We need to remind ourselves of the crucial nature of children's emotional attachments if we are to fully appreciate the far-reaching nature of their disruption in the periods leading up to, during, and following a divorce. All infants need to become attached to a parent (or parent substitute) in order to survive. The child's growing bonds of love and loyalty are a great source of joy to her/his mother and father. At the very foundation of normal development is the child's emotional tie to her/his parents and their bonding. Erik Erikson (1965) proposes that the essential task of infancy is the development of a basic trust in others. He believes that during the early months and years of life, children learn about security – whether the world is a good and satisfying place to live in, or a source of pain, misery, frustration and uncertainty. Because human infants are so totally dependent for so long, they need to know that they can depend on the outside world.

This trust, this sense of dependability, is sorely threatened during the time around a divorce. The separation(s) of child and parents, which are part of the pattern of divorce, take people to the far edge of suffering. Ralph Waldo Emerson observed perceptively that 'Sorrow makes us all children again'. Matters are not helped when indecisive parents separate, reunite, separate again … and so on. Children's hopes are cruelly raised, dashed and raised again.

Separation anxiety

A further turn of the screw comes from the potency of separation anxiety as part of the child's experience of normal (let alone disrupted) development. Children's fears show a clear pattern as they grow up – each age seems to have its own set of adjustment crises or anxieties. Studies of the behaviour of healthy children separated from their parents in the second and third years of life tend to show a fairly predictable sequence of behaviour, outlined as follows.

➤ In the first, or 'protest', stage children react to the separation – brought about, say, by their mother's hospitalization – with tears and anger. They demand their mother's return and seem hopeful that they will succeed in getting her back. This stage may last several days.

➤ Later they become quieter, but it is clear that they are just as preoccupied with their absent mother and still yearn for her return, although their hopes may have faded.

➤ This is called the phase of despair. Often the stages alternate: hope turns to despair, and despair to renewed hope.

➤ Eventually a greater change occurs: children seem to forget their mother so that, when they see her again, they remain curiously uninterested in her and may seem not to recognize her. This is the so-called stage of 'detachment'.

In each of these phases children are prone to tantrums and episodes of destructive behaviour. After reunion with their parents they may be unresponsive and undemanding, and to what degree and for how long depends on the length of the separation and whether or not they received frequent visits during that period. For example, if they have been deprived of visits for a good few weeks and have reached the early stages of detachment, it is likely that unresponsiveness will persist for varying periods, ranging from a few hours to several days. When at last this unresponsiveness subsides, the intense ambivalence of their feelings for their mother is made manifest. There can be a storm of feeling, intense clinging, and, whenever mother leaves them, even for a moment, acute anxiety and rage. Here is a mother speaking:

> Ever since I left her that time I had to go into hospital (two periods, 17 days each, when the child was aged two years), she doesn't trust me any more. I can't go anywhere – over to the neighbour's or to the shops – I've always got to take her. She wouldn't leave me. She ran like mad home. She said, 'Oh Mam, I thought you was gone!' She can't forget it. She's still round me all the time. I just sit down and put her on my knee and love her. Definitely. If I don't do it, she says 'Mam, you don't love me any more'; I've *got* to sit down.

If these are the reactions of a toddler to the brief loss of her mother, what of the child who has to face the dismantling of his/her home and the *permanent* loss of one of his/her parents? The intimations and fears of separation will be much greater. Richard Lansdown (1993) says that in talking to families in crisis over an impending permanent separation, such as an individual dying, and being mindful of the conflict at times of death between what is known intellectually and what is felt emotionally, he will ask:

'What do you think in your head and what do you feel in your heart?'

It is only too easy to equate the impact of some divorces, especially where children are concerned, with the ramifications of a death (see Lansdown and Benjamin, 1985). The same question is apposite for bemused, bereaved adults and children alike.

Part II: The first shock waves

Many couples ask themselves, 'How are we going to break the news to the children? We want to let them down as lightly as possible'. Because the wish to break away creates so much guilt in most parents, the moment of revelation is often delayed until it is no longer possible to conceal the imminent separation. Meantime the parents assume that the children are blind to what is going on, despite witnessing quarrels, overhearing remarks, noticing changes in parents' mood and behaviour. Conflict may have been going on for months, or even longer, and children may react in various ways to the uncertainties – behaviour problems, regressive clinging, weepiness, even bed-wetting and nightmares.

Clearly, there cannot be any rigid formula as to when to tell a child about the parents' decision to separate. But a long period of uncertainty, followed by an abrupt statement of intent, is harmful.

Pre-school children

Not surprisingly, pre-school children usually appear to be very sad and frightened when their parents actually separate, and they become very clinging and demanding. Bedtime fears and a refusal to be left alone, even for a few minutes, are not uncommon. Children attending school or nursery may become very anxious about going there, and may protest strongly when left. Vivid fantasies about abandonment, death of parents, or injury are encountered, and they often express aggression towards other children, and quarrel with brothers and sisters.

School-age children

With somewhat older children, grief and sadness remain a prominent feature, but anger becomes more marked. This is usually directed at the parents, especially the one with whom the child is living – which more often than not means the mother. ('Is there no justice?', she must sometimes ask herself.) Regardless of the actual events leading to the breakdown, she is likely to be blamed by the child for everything that has happened. The absent father is quite likely to be idealized (again, regardless of realities) while the mother is held responsible for driving him away. Children, especially in the age group seven to eight, may express very strong yearnings for their father.

Pre-adolescent children

Pre-adolescent children tend to demonstrate less of their inner hurt and distress, which is not to say that it does not exist. Covering up is common and they may seek distractions in play and other activities, in the way that an adult might seek solace in alcohol or frenetic busyness. It may be difficult to get through to children at this age; they are loath to talk about what they are feeling because of the pain and embarrassment it causes them. Underneath this apparent detachment is anger, and again, they may align themselves very strongly with one parent and even refuse to see the other.

Adolescents

Adolescents sometimes show overt depression and appear to 'opt out' of family life and withdraw into other relationships outside the home. Friends may become the alternative to the family, providing a sense of belonging, continuity and stability. Some friends may be an undesirable influence, providing the excitement in mischief or hell-raising that acts as an antidote to the youngster's misery. Worries about their own relationships, sex and marriage may surface (see Wallerstein and Kelly, 1980).

These are the immediate and middle-term reactions to parental separation. The 'grief work' is very much like that of a bereavement. Usually the reactions are seen in an acute form for a matter of months and then, hopefully, will begin to subside. Unfortunately, the evidence concerning long-term consequences is still rather meagre and difficult to evaluate (see Wallerstein, 1985; 1991).

Some dos for the practitioner
(see Grollman, 1975; Wells, 1989)

Here are some ideas for helping the child to deal with his/her sense of loss.

Encourage the parent and child to communicate with each other. Silence, the hush of shock and sorrow, often enfold the child following a divorce/separation. This can be frightening and alienating.

Explore (using conversation, play, drawing, genograms and stories) how the child is thinking, feeling and acting. Any story which has loss as its theme may be suitable for helping children express their worries and emotions about the break-up of their home. You can may make up your own stories or use picture books or games to encourage communication (see the useful book edited by Patricia Scowne, *Supporting bereaved children and families,* 1993).

Most children are feeling somewhat better by the end of the first year following their loss, but the grieving process takes approximately two years in all, as for adults, and longer for sudden, unexpected disasters. Of course, this does not preclude the return of the pain of sadness and yearning, especially at anniversary, holiday or other special times, or when the child is ill. Reminders of family events and traditions – no longer possible – are hard to bear.

It is important to:

➤ be available to the family if you have been asked to intervene; keep in touch;
➤ listen; give the child permission to express as much of their sadness (and other feelings) as they are willing to share at the time;
➤ encourage them to talk about the divorce and their sense of loss;
➤ normalize their feelings; accept them; explain to them why they are feeling this way, if necessary;
➤ be honest and open with questions;
➤ ask children what help/support they would like;
➤ ask parents what help/support they would like;
➤ share, by talking, good and not-so-good family memories (for example, look at family photograph albums with them);
➤ be prepared to discuss practical matters which may be crucial to the family's adjustment;
➤ encourage the parent to communicate to the child the fact that s/he is not alone or in danger of being abandoned.

Difficulties in coming to terms with loss

It is common in divorce courts to find children reacting to separation/divorce in ways which are unadaptive. These include:

➤ *Helplessness.* The child may 'opt out' of family and school life. This is a psychological defence mechanism called 'emotional insulation'.

> *Aggression.* The child may act out inner hurt, resentment, confusion or turmoil by hitting out at the world.
> *Substitution.* The child may seek out a substitute father or mother.

Ideas to help/support the child

> Watch for verbalizations and behaviour changes that suggest problems; for example, self-blame, persistent depression, aggressive, antisocial behaviour.
> Provide boltholes for privacy, a place for the child to express emotions or be quietly alone.
> Give time and attention: listen.
> Tackle the difficult subjects, such as parental incompatibility; be honest with questions.
> Involve the child's special friends if the child is becoming isolated.
> Be mindful of special days.
> Suggest s/he might write letters to or telephone an absent parent – but be mindful of contact and access arrangements!

Some don'ts for the practitioner

> **Don't** advise the family members not to worry or not to be sad.
> **Don't** advise them as to what they should feel.
> **Don't** say you know how they feel … you don't!
> **Don't** say, 'You should be adjusting by now'.
> **Don't** say, 'At least you still have a mother/father at home'.
> **Don't** deny their point of view (for example, anger, resentment).
> **Don't** encourage parents to hide their grief from their child. Say, 'It is alright to cry in front of your child'.
> **Don't** say 'Your daddy/mummy may come back soon'.
> **Don't** neglect to liaise with the child's school. Children, when distressed, may misbehave (act out) and/or underachieve due to poor concentration, apathy, or low motivation (as part of a feeling of depression). Teachers may not be fully aware of the reasons.

The fall-out

One of the questions of concern to parents is the long-term effect of divorce on the child's mental health. As I mentioned earlier, researchers have found that those people who experience a broken home in childhood have a higher risk of developing psychological problems over the longer term, compared with those from unbroken homes. For those from a comfortable economic background, there is no difference at all in the risk factor. Indeed, children from broken homes may fare better than youngsters from *unhappy, unbroken* homes!

These findings, however, do not allow us to be at all complacent. The relatively reassuring information about the effects of broken homes on psychiatric illness in later life is not repeated in the area of delinquency. Here the influences are more malign, given certain aggravating circumstances. Delinquency is associated with the break-up of homes where there has been a great deal of parental disharmony; the association is not with the disruption of the home, as such. The loss of a parent through a marital separation is much more likely to cause long-term problems than a loss through death. This may be because of the unpleasant events that often precede the break-up or because the child experiences a feeling of betrayal, of some intentional abandonment.

Contact with parents

What we do not yet know for certain is whether the long-term ill-effects are reduced if a child remains in contact with both parents after a break. Indirect evidence indicates that this condition may be important. Among the longer-term problems associated with divorce and separation are depression, low self-esteem, problems in heterosexual relations (especially for girls), difficulties on assuming parenthood, and an increased likelihood of divorce in the youngster's own marriage. There are many question marks over the precise significance and extent of these effects, but we *can* be sure that if at all present, the differences between children from a background of divorce and those with no such background are relatively small. Much depends on influences such as the quality of the child's relationship with each parent and how these change after the separation.

Wallerstein and Kelly (1980) suggest, on the basis of their work, that parents generally express their anger more openly with the older youngsters, and try to shield the youngest children from the worst of the bitterness. Thus the older youngster, the nine- to eighteen-year-olds, are frequently more upset, and their distress continues parallel to their parents' anger. They also found that in some cases the older boys and girls tended to identify with the humiliation and feelings of rejection that overwhelmed their angry mothers, and hence were more distressed and upset by the anger and bitterness the mother expressed toward the father. Similarly, older boys were particularly upset and preoccupied with the divorce when they believed that their father had been 'thrown out'. The anxiety of these children, as well as their ongoing desire for a reconciliation between their parents, was significantly linked to the parent's damaged self-esteem.

Wallerstein and Kelly also found that, in general, parenting of the younger children was better sustained by both parents than parenting of the older children. Their results revealed that children from the age of nine upwards were keenly aware of the decline in the quality of parenting and felt wronged and neglected. The majority of the nine- and ten-year-old boys they interviewed felt that their fathers were unavailable to them and were intensely hurt by the experience. In the same way, the older girls felt emotionally abandoned by their mothers at this critical time when their need for support was paramount.

They also report that the gap between parents and children at the time of separation was widened still further by the increased irritability and emotional turmoil of the older children, two-thirds of whom became more difficult to manage. In their preoccupation with their own feelings and reactions, the divorced parents found the intense anger felt by the older children extremely frustrating and discouraging. On the other hand, the demanding and clinging behaviour of the younger children, and their reluctance to allow the custodial parent out of their sight for fear that s/he might not return, served only to further deplete the resources of already fatigued parents.

Perhaps one of the most disturbing findings reported by Wallerstein and Kelly, and principally found in the nine- to twelve-year-old range, was the alignment of the child with one parent. They define alignment as:

> '... the most extreme identification with the parent's cause – a divorce-specific relationship that occurs when a parent and one or more children join in a vigorous attack on the other parent.' (Wallerstein and Kelly, 1980, p. 77).

The authors state that this finding also strongly suggests that the adults and children who join in these unhealthy alliances lack psychological stability, and the youngsters who join one parent in opposition against the other are exceptionally distressed at the time of the separation and feel particularly vulnerable as a result of the divorce. They found that the length of time that such alignments lasted was related to the custodial arrangements. Alignments with the father or the non-custodial parent in most cases did not persist beyond the first post-separation year. Maternal alignments, however, or alignments with the custodial parent, were found to be still strikingly stable eighteen months after the separation.

Overall, alignments with the custodial parent appeared to be the most lasting, and this might reflect not only the strength of the underlying feelings, but also the daily reinforcement of the bond. The not unreasonable suggestion is made that for many parents these anger-impelled campaigns against the other spouse might be a means of warding off impending depression.

Wallerstein and Kelly found that the only group of youngsters in their sample who did *not* suffer the characteristic profound loneliness after the separation were those well-functioning adolescents whose capacity to rely upon peers for entertainment and support was quite good, and those who enjoyed their father's continued interest. Furthermore, they state that although children of *all* ages experienced important changes in the relationship with their parents at this time of separation and divorce, the adolescent response is so inextricably interwoven with their relationship with their parents that the two have to be considered together.

The authors found that the impact of divorce either drives adolescent development forward at a greatly accelerated rate or brings it to a grinding halt. Those children whose maturity was accelerated (about one-third of their sample) generally moved quickly into protective and helpful roles and took on the sharing of household responsibility and the care of young siblings with competence, sensitivity and pride. Parents were able to depend upon these adolescents for companionship, for advice, for the sharing of major decisions, and for their very real help. Again, more markedly in late adolescence, these youngsters, to all intents and purposes, assumed something of a parental role.

Having to choose

Sadly, children may be forced to take sides. They all too frequently become the battlegrounds for marital warfare and are a tempting target for mutual recriminations about such things as neglect, favouritism or 'bad blood'. Being powerless, they are ideal scapegoats at a time when the parents feel miserable and frustrated. As the offspring of the disliked (possibly hated) spouse, the child can reflect qualities which are annoying in the marriage partner. This brand of unreason arises from the prolonged nature of the tensions and hostility of an unhappy marriage; the pressure on adults who have to live in close proximity, despite their incompatibility, makes them do and say spiteful and vicious things which they would not permit themselves to do or say under normal circumstances. The demand for a child to 'choose' between them is particularly invidious.

When a child is put under pressure, s/he may, in order to protect her/himself, play a 'You-are-the-one-I-like best' game and, for example, show preference for the parent s/he lives with. This game can be played as long as the child can avoid meeting both parents together. Family therapy, where all members of the family are confronted with one another, makes such games less possible for all concerned. The child who has used these tactics for some time will need help to find new ways of relating to his/her parents and vice versa.

Part III: The one left behind

Single parenthood

The number of mothers and fathers bringing up their children in single parent households (for many reasons other than divorce) is on the increase. The problems they face are somewhat similar whether they are separated, divorced, widowed or unmarried: finding enough energy and hours in the day to cope with a thousand and one chores. The lack of emotional support, the occasional morale booster, can be sorely missed when one bears the responsibility all alone for rearing children. There is a rather special apprehension for many divorced parents, especially mothers. What harm, they wonder, will come of the traumatic experiences the children have lived through? Will the difficulty of rearing boys and girls (particularly the former) unaided, be too much for me?

The generalities about the consequences of broken homes do not take into account the individual's suffering. Whatever the long-term statistical trends, we are still left with the intense and immediate (even if temporary) grief, confusion and apprehension which affect many children in the period leading up to and following the divorce. And the parent left behind has to cope with this. Fathers may feel they lack the intuitive touch – the understanding sensitivity of women. Mothers tend to worry over disciplinary problems, especially when the child finds an outlet in aggressive behaviour.

Economic factors

Economic factors are also vitally important; there is a close association between fatherlessness and poverty, and many of the unfavourable consequences of deprivation of a father are primarily the consequences of poverty. Poverty puts a mother under great strain. A prolonged period of difficulty leading up to the finality of divorce may leave the mother feeling depressed, and mentally and physically drained. Financial strain may exhaust the last emotional reserves of the mother left alone and for women in this predicament, housing is particularly difficult to find. Children under five years of age need special care and close attention. However, if the mother is short of money, she may be forced to seek employment without finding satisfactory substitute care; and this sometimes leads to inadequate protection and supervision of the child. Mothers often lose their social life as well as their emotional and physical support when deprived of their husbands. Given all these factors, it is scarcely surprising that some women question their resourcefulness and adequacy to cope with all the responsibilities of rearing children alone.

Other factors

Single parent families carry the risk of being somewhat claustrophobic, especially if the parent, out of sheer desolation, clings to the child and makes too many emotional demands of him/her ('Kim is like a sister – she goes everywhere with me' or, 'Peter is the man of the house now; I have him to lean on'). The continual attempt to compensate the child for her loss – 'I feel so guilty, I must make it up to him/her' – is usually misguided, frequently leading to spoiling and a self-centred, unappealing youngster.

As so many families have only one parent nowadays, it is just as well that children brought up by one adult are just as likely to be as psychologically 'healthy' as those reared in the more common pattern. Nevertheless mothers are particularly worried about the problem of being mother *and* 'father' to their child. For example, they may sometimes get concerned, about the normal development of their son's masculinity. To reassure mothers, it should be emphasized that a boy will not be confused about his gender simply because he grows up without a man about the house. If he lacks a model of his own sex within the home he is likely to have many in the family (for example, uncles), the school (teachers), and in the outside world (peers), to learn from.

Resilience

Parents should not be discouraged by the set-backs and traumas that beset children. One of the lessons for parents is that it is within their grasp, with or without professional help, to assist their children in their attempts to adapt to this and others of the inevitable vicissitudes of life. Children are learners and parents are their teachers; resourceful, imaginative teachers can help youngsters master the challenges and overcome the setbacks essential to his/her long-term well-being.

Several studies (as we have seen) suggest that a very good relationship with one of the parents is associated with better outcomes in children from divorced families. Grandparents living in the home are also a protective influence (see Garmezy and Masten, 1994). What impresses me after many years of having had the privilege of working with children, is their essentially robust quality and their remarkable capacity to find a viable response to adversity.

Part IV: Those on the edge of the abyss

Considering the child

All this may sound somewhat academic in relation to those parents who are teetering on the edge of the abyss of a breakup, but who are, quite rightly, considering the best interests of their children. It *is* so often a 'messy' and miserable outcome whatever parents choose – staying together or parting. They cannot escape, by rationalization, the fact that separation will inflict pain on the children. Every child would prefer to go on living with two happy parents. However, if they cannot find a peaceful and viable way of living together, they are doing their child no service by staying together for his/ her sake. If the sad and often tawdry aspects of divorce can be mitigated by sensitive handling by parents who put the children's interests before their own, the youngster will at least know that their mother and father care about what happens to them. This is where careful thought and planning about the future, perhaps with the assistance of a counsellor, become essential (see Goldstein, 1987).

Following the decision to separate, children should be informed as soon as possible, so that there is no risk of them hearing the news from someone else. It may be helpful, although small comfort, to know that most families go through a transition period of two or three years before they settle down to their new way of life. Wise parents might adopt the philosophical attitude that although they have failed as husband and wife to make a success of their marriage, they can at least try, for the sake of their children, to make a success of its termination and aftermath. A lot is at stake! The Virginia Longitudinal Study of Divorce and Remarriage (Hetherington et al., 1985) followed up a sample of families with a four-year-old child for six years after divorce had taken place. Considerable distress and dysfunction were observed in both parents and children over the first year. Boys appeared to have the most difficulty, manifested by aggressive, noncompliant ('externalizing') behaviour, and troubled mother–son relationships were evidenced during the second year. The girls' behaviour was similar to their comparison counterparts (those from non-divorced families). Compared to children in conflict-full non-divorced families, children from divorced families were initially worse off; but at the two year follow-up, they were better adjusted than children remaining within families notable by very unhappy marital relationships.

Step-parents

When a child's parent remarries – and they usually do – there may be problems of adjustment. The difficulties of being a step-child are legendary and so are the problems of being a step-parent in the growing number of reconstituted families. Research studies have confirmed these legends. Psychological evidence suggests that remarriage inflicts some degree of trauma on all children in this situation. Researchers have found that children living in households where remarriage has taken place experience greater levels of uncertainty of feelings, insecurity of position and strain than comparison groups. A majority of the original divorced sample in the Virginia study eventually remarried. Boys and girls in recently reconstituted families had significant externalizing problems, especially young adolescents. After two years of remarriage, behaviour appeared to improve for both boys and girls.

This issue is not a simple one, particularly as it has been shown that the presence or absence of post-divorce conflict between the parents exerts a greater influence on children's subsequent adjustment than does the marital status of a parent (see Emery, 1982; 1988). There is an increased risk of psychological problems where it is the parent of the same sex as the child who finds a new spouse. These findings are statistical, and reflect a slightly increased risk only. There are, of course, many instances of step-parents who have brought great happiness and solace to the children they adopt. The friction, jealousy and ambivalence which are a common feature of step-child–step-parent relationships can be overcome with thoughtful and empathetic handling. This means trying to see things from the child's point of view – the most imaginative thing a parent can do. For example, if the step-child lets him/herself go, and calls his/her step-father 'Daddy' and shows him affection, might s/he not lose the love of his/her real father because of his/her disloyalty? If s/he *does* accept the new situation, is s/he not admitting finally that his/her parents are not going to change their minds and have a reconciliation? These are some of the dilemmas the child faces, and the step-parent him/herself is not immune from conflict. They may ask themselves, 'To what extent should I try to be a mother when Carol still has a mother?; Am I as the step-father permitted to discipline this child?' There are books written by 'insiders' suggesting means of dealing with such issues (for example, Marshall, 1993, and Maddox, 1980).

More devastating than the fear of jealousy aroused by remarriage may be the fear of abandonment felt by a child whose parents allow a succession of romantic attachments to take priority over their relationship with their child.

Softening the blow

For some children, the disruption may be minimized by parents who can arrange that their children are protected from the more unpleasant features of the deteriorating marriage. Ideally, contact with the departed parent should be frequent, and free of the jealousy and competition for affection which beset so many post-divorce arrangements. Sadly, especially where there has been domestic violence, access may be poisonous in atmosphere and risky in execution.

Support systems

In the period both preceding and following a divorce, such factors as the child's resilience, the resourcefulness of the parent s/he remains with, the presence of fond grandparents or brothers and sisters who absorb some of the shock, all influence the outcome of the child's tragedy. As mentioned earlier, several studies (for example, Emery, 1982) suggest that a good relationship with one of the parents is associated with better outcomes in children from divorced families.

A long drawn-out trial period of reconciliation, breakdown, re-reconciliation and further separation, in which the child's hopes rise and fall, rise again and finally are dashed, causes more harm than a decisive resolution of conflict after quiet, private and careful consideration of their marriage by the parents. They may find it helpful to consult a neutral but understanding person such as a marriage guidance counsellor, or religious adviser. There are excellent books such as Marge Heegard's *When Mom and Dad Separate* (1991), to help children learn to cope with the grief that follows divorce.

The child's best interests

You may like to know what children have said about divorce. Their comments help define their best interests. Yvette Walczak's (1984) study is of great interest here, because, unlike most researchers, she has looked at divorce through the eyes of 100 people (adults and children) who had been at the receiving end. She found that of the factors that were significant to a benign outcome for children after all the misery of a divorce, three were of the utmost significance. These were:

1.   communication about separation;
2.   continued good relationship with at least one parent;
3.   satisfaction with custody and access arrangements.

Children who considered themselves most damaged were:

➤   those whose parents were not able to talk to them about divorce, apart from blaming their ex-spouse;
➤   those who did not get on well with at least one parent after separation;
➤   those who were dissatisfied with custody and access arrangements, whatever these happened to be.

Most children would have liked two happily married parents, but most preferred to live with a single parent than with two unhappily married ones.

Parenting after marriage ends

Walczak also sees a need for a change of public attitude and legislation. The Children Act, 1989 (published after her paper) attends to some of the issues, in general, of parental responsibility and children's welfare that she raises (see Herbert, 1993). Parenting *after* the marriage ends needs to receive as much recognition and attention as parenting *within* marriage has so far received. In marriage both parents are recognized as legal custodians of their children. Walczak wishes to see joint custody being the rule, and custody to one parent an exception, with, whenever possible, the parents discussing, agreeing, and submitting joint proposals of arrangements for their children's future.

Setting tasks for surviving the divorce

Wallerstein (1985; 1991) has reported on a ten-year follow-up of her original sample. In these, and other publications, she illustrates the complex problems and opportunities posed by divorce. At this ten-year follow-up, the psychological tasks facing adults and children at the time of divorce are set out.

Divorce was perceived as setting two sets of tasks for the adults involved. The first was to rebuild their lives as adults so as to make good use of the second chances that the divorce provided. The second task was to parent the children after divorce, protecting them from the crossfire between the former partners, and nurturing them as they grew up. The adult tasks were as follows:

➤ Ending the marriage.
➤ Mourning the loss.
➤ Reclaiming oneself.
➤ Resolving or containing passions.
➤ Rebuilding.
➤ Helping the children through:
  1. pre-school;
  2. the early school years – five to eight;
  3. the later school years – nine to twelve; and
  4. adolescence.

Once the decision to divorce was made, the following were perceived as important as a means of helping the children.

➤ The expression of sadness was important because it gave children permission to cry and mourn without having to hide their feelings of loss from the adults or from themselves.
➤ Rationality was important because it contributed to the child's moral development.
➤ Clarity was important so that children would not be encouraged to undertake any efforts at reconciliation.
➤ Reluctance was important because children needed to feel that parents were aware of how profoundly upset the children would be.
➤ If true, the parents could say that the children had been one of the greatest pleasures of the marriage.
➤ Parents needed to prepare children for what lay ahead in as much specific detail as possible.

➤ Courage was a good word to use when explaining divorce to children. It was important that the parents emphasized that everyone concerned would have to be brave.

➤ Children needed to be reassured by being given the assurance that they would be kept informed of all major developments.

➤ Because children felt so completely powerless in the divorce situation, they should be invited to make suggestions that the adults would seriously consider.

➤ Children needed to be told, over and over again, that the divorce did not weaken the bond between non-custodial parent and child, despite the fact that they would now live apart.

➤ Parents needed to give the children permission to love both parents freely and openly.

Wallerstein is of the opinion that the psychological tasks for the children were:

➤ understanding the divorce;

➤ strategic withdrawal – children and adolescents needed to return to living their own lives as soon as possible after the divorce. It was very important for them to recommence their usual activities at school and at play and to return both physically and emotionally to the normal tasks of growing up;

➤ dealing with loss;

➤ dealing with anger;

➤ working through and resolving guilt;

➤ accepting the permanence of divorce; and

➤ taking a chance on love – it was most important that children should not feel unlovable because of the divorce. They should be encouraged to accept realistically that they could both love and be loved.

Part V: Counselling divorced parents

A counselling and life skills training programme

These programmes can be of benefit to separated/divorced parents, particularly to the one who is the children's main caregiver. The following programme in broad outline can be effective with recently divorced mothers and/or fathers; the outline is deliberately broad so that you can incorporate your own ideas and strategies.

Goals

The important changes that take place after divorce suggest the following goals for group or individual work:

➤ adjustment to being single after being one of a couple;
➤ being the sole head of a single-parent family with the main, and often sole, responsibility, for disciplining and caring for the children;
➤ frequently having to leave the familiar family home to set up house in an unfamiliar neighbourhood;
➤ making new, and losing old, friends;
➤ often having to deal with some degree of impoverishment and having to cope with the disruption of family life;
➤ often coping with children's emotional and behavioural problems.

The life-skills component of a course designed by Joy Edelstein (in association with the author) draws heavily on suggestions from the work of Hopson and Scally (1980). They point out that what underlies the concept of self-empowerment is the belief that there are alternatives available in any situation; the skill is being able to select one of them on the basis of personal values, priorities and commitments. Edelstein (1996) was able to demonstrate that this version of a counselling and lifeskills training programme, by helping the maternal participants to achieve better adjustment and greater self-empowerment, facilitated a degree of recovery from the ill-effects of divorce. Further, this improved maternal coping and functioning served to alleviate, in some measure, the damaging effects of divorce upon the children.

Course content (see p. 29 for sources of materials)

Session 1: Orientation

In this session, the participants are introduced to each other and to the programme facilitator. The approach adopted by the group leader(s) stresses that divorce is a major life event which is transitional in nature; that it *is* possible to train people to cope more effectively with the transitions in their lives, and that, because children are the parents of tomorrow, it is of the utmost importance to alleviate divorce-related emotional and other problems that affect them.

Session 2: Reassurance for the children

This session focuses on ways parents can reassure their children. It details the reactions children have to divorce, the defence mechanisms, such as denial, and 'acting-out' behaviour, such as aggression, they employ to stave off the hurt and resentment they feel as they work through the trauma of divorce. Methods for managing the working through or acting out behaviours that children frequently display are discussed and debated at this session.

Session 3: Reassurance for the divorced person

This session focuses on providing reassurance for the participants themselves. It includes a description of common (immediate) reactions to the break-up and emphasizes that such reactions are normal; it also recognizes the possible need in some cases to 'mourn' a lost marriage. There are suggestions on how to cope with the loneliness that follows a divorce and on ways of handling self-doubt; this session stresses the importance of combating the resentment and bitterness that stem from a broken marriage and outlines constructive ways that participants can help themselves face the future on their own.

Session 4: (a) Looking after yourself
(b) Confronting some thorny issues

The ideas of supportive self-talk and the expression of feelings are introduced, and the concept of 'appropriateness' is explained. Skills for managing emotions are described, as are criteria for adequate self-care. Group members participate in a relaxation exercise. The thorny issues of custody, child maintenance and access are confronted and ways of dealing with frustrating access problems are discussed and debated.

Session 5: (a) Letting go of the past
(b) Hints for managing difficult childhood behaviours

Pointers are given for explaining divorce to children. The essential step of letting go of the past once the grief of a broken marriage has been worked through, is underlined as a fundamental element of emotional recovery. The irrational beliefs and attributions that people harbour are examined and techniques for venting anger constructively discussed. Parents are helped to pinpoint, observe and record unwanted childhood behaviours. In the second half of the session the advantages of examining behaviours in terms of the problem-solving ABC of behaviour method (Herbert, 1987) is discussed.

Session 6: (a) 'Know yourself'
(b) More hints for managing difficult childhood behaviours

The important self-knowledge questions, 'Would I have chosen for this to have happened?' and, 'Do I know what I want from this new situation?' are posed and debated. The first question leaves the individual with three possible options, namely, accept and put up with the situation; refuse to accept the situation; or, accept the situation and try to benefit from it. The effects of these options are carefully examined and the usefulness of the key question, 'What is the worst that can happen?' explored.

The second question, 'Do I know what I want from this new situation?', is used to introduce the technique of *values clarification* as a means of crystallizing needs and values, and the differing consequences of proactive and reactive behaviour are discussed.

Stress control techniques are described and practised (see Herbert, 1987) during this session.

In the second half of the session, more hints for managing difficult childhood behaviours are given, and also on managing the consequences outlined (see Webster-Stratton and Herbert, 1994). In addition, effective ways of using rewards and penalties, and encouraging good attending behaviour, are discussed.

A list of parenting skills (see *Appendix I) is* used as a handout for parents to think about at home and for discussion later.

Session 7: (a) 'Knowing and understanding your new situation'
(b) Taboo corner: dating, sex, and the single parent

In 'Knowing your new situation', the importance of recognizing the meaning and dynamics of *transition* as a prerequisite to coping with it, is discussed and the individual's movement through the stages of transition described. Self-empowerment skills are examined, focusing on the four types of skills required, namely:

➤ My skills: skills I need to survive and grow generally;
➤ Me-and-you skills: skills I need to relate effectively to you;
➤ Me and others: skills I need to relate effectively to others; and,
➤ Me and specific situations: skills I need for my education, skills I need at work, skills I need at home, skills I need at leisure and skills I need in the community (see *Appendix I*).

In 'Taboo corner', it is stressed that just because a person is divorced does not mean that s/he has stopped being human or experiencing human needs. The sensitive issues of dating and sex in the context of single parenthood, and the effects of parental dating on the children are carefully examined. The dangers of exposing children to frequent attachment–separation experiences, as is the case if parents introduce a number of opposite-sex friends or lovers (or same-sex, as the case may be) into the family unit, are explored.

Session 8: (a) 'Knowing other people who can help'
(b) More hints for managing difficult childhood behaviours

The importance of finding other people to talk with about problems (in the absence of the spouse) after divorce, is emphasized. How to give and receive feedback is also discussed.

In the latter half of the session, which deals with more hints for managing difficult childhood behaviours, the antecedents are discussed, with particular attention to situations that seem to trigger

difficult behaviours. In this context, hints are given for anticipati
trouble and planning to avoid it.

Session 9:   (a) Learning from the past
(b) The principles of good communication
(c) More about managing difficult
childhood behaviours

How we learn from specific experiences and the fact that there is a
learning potential in both positive and negative experiences is teased
out by brain-storming. The principles of effective communication
are outlined and the role of communication in making and maintaining
relationships discussed. The skills of sending and receiving messages
are examined in some detail. A model of communication is presented
and obstacles to effective communication considered. Effective
parent–child communication is described with emphasis on the skill
of reflecting the child's feelings. The effectiveness of appropriate self-
disclosure is illustrated.

   In the latter half of the session, dealing with the management of
difficult childhood behaviours, and ways of extending the behavioural
approach to other behaviours in the child's repertoire are discussed,
with the suggestion that other unwanted childhood behaviours be
recorded. Categories of difficult childhood behaviours are
brainstormed and listed and ways of maintaining improvement in a
child's behaviour suggested (see *Appendices II* and *III*).

Session 10: (a) Self-empowerment and how to learn
from experience
(b) How to be assertive

The belief underlying the concept of self-empowerment, namely, 'No
matter what, there is always an alternative we can choose', is
brainstormed. The five dimensions defining self-empowerment:
awareness, goals, values, lifeskills and information, are discussed and
debated (see Webster-Stratton and Herbert, 1994). How to learn from
experience, how to make decisions, and how to be assertive are
outlined. Group members participate in an assertiveness exercise.

Session 11: (a) Being positive about oneself
(b) Problem-solving

The importance of enjoying healthy self-regard and the beneficial
effects of having positive self-esteem are examined. The experience of

being a winner or a loser, and the effects on the individual of achieving success or suffering failure, are considered. Positive self-talk in particular is outlined. The nature of problem-solving is explained and a model of problem-solving presented (Hopson and Scally, 1980). The idea of creative problem-solving is introduced and the skills that need to be acquired for effective problem-solving are outlined and debated. The group members participate in a problem-solving exercise.

Session 12: (a) 'Gains you have made'
(b) Participants' presentation
(c) Termination of the programme: saying goodbye

The participants complete a Likert scale-type *Gains Questionnaire* that provides a range of options indicating degrees of improvement, change or deterioration in interpersonal skills and lifeskills dealt with in the training programme. The participants then present *their* ideas on what should be included in an effective counselling and lifeskills training programme for divorced persons. A short video-film on divorce and its impact is screened, and an informative lecture on custody and access, with question time, is presented. This is followed by a short farewell address by the group leaders who thank parents for their participation and remind them of the follow-up meeting to be arranged in six months. A special tea brings the meeting to a close.

Mid-session breaks

A short break is given midway through each session to allow participants to leave the room for various purposes, such as a chat and a chance to relax or reflect.

Major sources of the content material used

In addition to the influence of Hopson and Scally (1980) on the material dealing with the teaching of lifeskills, the material for the management of difficult childhood behaviours comes largely from the project conducted at the Parent Skills Group meetings by Jenny Wookey and Martin Herbert (methods are described in Herbert, 1993; Webster-Stratton and Herbert, 1994; and Wookey and Herbert, 1996). The material on divorce issues is gleaned from a number of sources: principally the work of Garmezy and Masten (1994); Goldstein (1987); Hetherington *et al.* (1985); Stuart and Abt (1981); and Wallerstein and Kelly (1980).

A proforma for describing problem areas to work with is provided in *Appendix IV*.

Conclusion

The negative aspects of divorce have been emphasized in this guide. It should not be forgotten that, although grief is an important feature in divorce, some marriages do come to an end quite calmly, with the separating couple taking a calm and rational decision to go their separate ways and possibly feeling greatly relieved to do so.

References

Cantor, D. and Drake, E. (1983). *Divorced Parents and Their Children: A guide for mental health professionals*. New York: Springer.

Cherlin, A.J., Furstenberg, F.F., Chase-Lansdale, P.L., Kiernan, K.E., Robins, P.K., Morrison, D.R., and Teitler, J.O. (1991). Longitudinal studies of divorce on children in Great Britain and the United States. *Science*, *252*, 1386–1389.

Edelstein, J. (1996). *Psycho-social Consequences of Divorce: A group counselling programme of prevention*. Unpublished PhD thesis, University of Leicester.

Emery, R.E. (1982). Interparental conflict and the children of discord and divorce. *Psychological Bulletin*, *92*, 310–330.

Emery, R.E. (1988). *Marriage: Divorce and Children's Adjustment*. Newbury Park, CA: Sage.

Erikson, E. (1965). *Childhood and Society*. Harmondsworth: Penguin.

Garmezy, N. and Masten, A.S. (1994). Chronic adversities. In M. Rutter *et al.* (Eds) *Child and adolescent psychiatry*. Oxford: Blackwell.

Goldstein, S. (1987). *Divorce parenting: How to make it work*. London: Methuen.

Grollman, E.A. (1975). *Talking about Divorce*. Boston: Beacon Press.

Heegaard, M. (1991). *When Mom and Dad Separate: Children can learn to cope with grief from divorce*. Minneapolis: Woodland Press.

Herbert, M. (1987). *Behavioural Treatment of Children with Problems*. London: Academic Press.

Herbert, M. (1993). *Working with Children and the Children Act*. Leicester: BPS Books (The British Psychological Society).

Hetherington, E.M., Cox, M. and Cox, R. (1985). Long term effects of divorce and remarriage on the adjustment of children. *Journal of the American Academy of Child Psychiatry*, *24*, 518–530.

Holmes, T.H. and Rahe, R.H. (1967). Social Readjustment Rating Scale. *Journal of Psychosomatic Research*, *11*, 213–218.

Hopson, B., and Scally, M. (1980). *Lifeskills Teaching: Education for self-empowerment*. New York: McGraw-Hill.

Jewett, C. (1982). *Helping Children Cope with Separation and Loss*. London: Batsford. **(Material in *Hints for Parents 2* is based on Claudia Jewett's work.)**

Lansdown, R. (1993). The development of the concept of death in children. In: P. Scowne (Ed.) *Supporting Bereaved Children and Families*. London: CRUSE-Bereavement Care.

Lansdown, R. and Benjamin, G. (1985). The development of the concept of death in children aged 5–9 years. *Child Care, Health and Development*, *11*, 13–20.

Maddox, B. (1980). *Step-Parenting: How to Live with Other People's Children*. London: Unwin.

Rutter, M. and Madge, N. (1976). *Cycles of Disadvantage*. London: Heinemann.

Scowne, P. (1993). *Supporting Bereaved Children and Families*. London: CRUSE-Bereavement Care.

Stuart, I.R. and Abt, L.E. (1981). *Children of Separation and Divorce: Management and treatment*. New York: Van Nostrand and Reinhold.

Walczak, Y. (1984). Divorce, the kids' stories. *Social Work Today*, *18 June*, 12–13.

Wallerstein, J. (1985). Children of divorce: Preliminary report of a ten-year follow-up of older children and adolescents. *Journal of the American Academy of Child Psychiatry*, *24*, 545–553.

Wallerstein, J. (1991). The long-term effects of divorce on children: A review. *Journal of the American Academy of Child Psychiatry*, *30*, 349–360.

Wallerstein, J. and Kelly, J.B. (1980). *Surviving the Break-up: How children and parents cope with divorce*. New York: Basic Books.

Ward, B. and Associates (1993). *Good grief: exploring feelings, loss and death. Volume 1: With under elevens; Volume 2: With over elevens and adults*. London: Jessica Kingsley Publishers.

Webster-Stratton, C. and Herbert, M. (1994). *Troubled Families: Problem children*. Chichester: Wiley.

Wells, R. (1989). *Helping Children Cope with Divorce*. London: Sheldon.

Wookey, J. and Herbert, M. (1996). *The Wookey–Herbert Parent Skills Manual*. In preparation.

Further reading

Burrett, J. (1991). *To and Fro Children: A guide to successful parenting after divorce.* London: Thorsons.
Hetherington, E.M., Stanley-Hagan, M. and Anderson, E.R. (1989). Marital transitions: a child's perspective. *American Psychologist, 44*, 303–312.
Marshall, P. (1993). *Cinderella Revisited: How to Survive your Stepfamily Without a Fairy Godmother.* Leicester: BPS Books (The British Psychological Society). This book has an excellent reading list for children and adults.

The National STEPFAMILY Association can be contacted at Chapel House, 18 Hatton Place, London EC1N 8RU.

Appendix I: A list of parenting skills

(Adapted from Hopson and Scally, 1980)

Me and my child	Me and significant others
Skills I need to relate effectively to him/her	*Skills I need to relate effectively to others (e.g. my partner, teachers, friends) involved with my child*
How to communicate clearly	How to be reasonably objective about others
How to listen carefully so as to understand	How not to be possessive
How to develop my relationship	How to be assertive (without being intrusive or bossy)
How to give help and care and protection without 'going over the top'	How to influence crucial people and systems (e.g. school)
How to teach and to discipline	How to work in groups (e.g. parents' groups, pressure groups)
How to show and receive affection	How to express my feelings clearly and constructively
How to manage/resolve conflict	How to inspire confidence and strength in others
How to give and receive feedback	
How to maintain a balance between extremes (e.g. loving without being possessive)	How to see my child's friends from his/her point of view
How to negotiate sensible compromises	How to resist/cope with jealousy
How to set reasonable limits and stick to them	

Appendix II: A child behaviour rating scale for parents

How much difficulty do you have with your child's behaviour on the following items? Circle the number that best sums up your opinion: 1 = never; 2 = sometimes; 3 = often. Indicate whether it represents a problem to you.

Behaviour	Never	Sometimes	Often	Do you see it as a problem?
Aggressiveness	1	2	3	Yes/No
Whining	1	2	3	Yes/No
Temper tantrums	1	2	3	Yes/No
Lying	1	2	3	Yes/No
Jealousy	1	2	3	Yes/No
Attention-demanding	1	2	3	Yes/No
Disobedience	1	2	3	Yes/No
Bedwetting	1	2	3	Yes/No
Daytime wetting	1	2	3	Yes/No
Shyness	1	2	3	Yes/No
Speech difficulties	1	2	3	Yes/No
Fears	1	2	3	Yes/No
School refusal	1	2	3	Yes/No
Soiling	1	2	3	Yes/No
Overactivity	1	2	3	Yes/No
Reading difficulty	1	2	3	Yes/No
Boredom	1	2	3	Yes/No
Apathy	1	2	3	Yes/No
Mood changes	1	2	3	Yes/No
Irritability	1	2	3	Yes/No
Wandering	1	2	3	Yes/No
Tics	1	2	3	Yes/No
Oversensitivity	1	2	3	Yes/No
Quarrelling	1	2	3	Yes/No
Poor/faddy eating	1	2	3	Yes/No
Timidity	1	2	3	Yes/No

Appendix III: A situational rating scale for parents

Do you have difficulty with your child at the following places or in the following circumstances? Circle the number that best sums up your opinion.

Place/circumstance	Never	Some-times	Often	Do you see it as a worrying problem?
Visiting friends	1	2	3	Yes/No
Shopping (e.g. supermarket)	1	2	3	Yes/No
Going on a bus	1	2	3	Yes/No
People visiting your home	1	2	3	Yes/No
Taking the child to school or nursery	1	2	3	Yes/No
Leaving the child at playgroup	1	2	3	Yes/No
Getting the child dressed	1	2	3	Yes/No
Mealtimes	1	2	3	Yes/No
Getting the child to bed	1	2	3	Yes/No
Getting the child to stay in bed	1	2	3	Yes/No
Quarrelling with brothers, sisters, friends	1	2	3	Yes/No
Getting the child to go to parties (friends' homes)	1	2	3	Yes/No
Getting the child to speak to people	1	2	3	Yes/No
Taking children's toys	1	2	3	Yes/No
Getting the child to share toys	1	2	3	Yes/No
Getting the child to be polite	1	2	3	Yes/No

Appendix IV: Clarifying problem areas

Client's name:
Date:

	Not a problem	A mild problem	A serious problem
1 Feeling low or depressed			
2 Feeling anxious			
3 So anxious I can't go out			
4 Having no friends			
5 Having money worries or debt			
6 Tensions with children			
7 Worries about children			
8 Worries about family members			
9 Sexual problems			
10 Worries about personal relationships at work or at home			
11 Tensions from cultural factors			
12 Housing problems			
13 Worries about alcohol use			
14 Worries about drug use			
15 Worries about things I've done wrong			
16 Worries about members of my family			
17 Worries about my health or mental health			
18 Worries about things I can't talk easily about			
19 Grieving for someone or something			
20 Something else			

Hints for Parents 1:
Children's grieving processes

Many children find it difficult to grieve. They may:

➢ refuse to accept the separation/divorce, dwelling on fantasies about reconciliation;
➢ have ambivalent feelings toward the parent who has left the home (and the remaining one);
➢ have doubts about the reality/finality of the separation;
➢ be reluctant to let themselves feel or express sorrow.
➢ have had a succession of losses that leave them feeling frozen or numb.

Some dos and don'ts for the parent

➢ Do permit (that is, understand and tolerate) children to go through their own individual stages of grieving.
➢ Do seek help from other supportive persons, such as friends.
➢ Do notify the child's school or day care centre about the child's distress and the reasons for it.
➢ Do encourage children to participate in your sorrow, if you are feeling it, but *not* your bitterness or recriminations.
➢ Do provide continued assurance of love and support – when words fail, touch.
➢ Don't discourage the subject of the divorce and separation in the home.
➢ Don't tell your children something that they will later need to unlearn, such as their father/mother will return.
➢ Don't put down the other parent in front of the child.
➢ Don't alter the role of the child, for example, making them a replacement for the departed parent.
➢ Don't speak about events at a level beyond the child's level of comprehension.
➢ Be frank and honest with the child within the limits of their level of comprehension.

Hints for Parents 2: Granting 'permission' to love the new family

It has been stated that the wise parent will not force the child to choose whom s/he likes best or which side s/he is on. In the case of a reconstituted family, the relinquishing parent gives the most precious gift to the child when s/he can wish the new parent well. Parents effectively give this permission when they take the time for the child to make a gradual transition to the new family setting, visiting them often before the final move.

A helpful technique, paraphrased here, for letting the child know that s/he can love a new family, without giving up her/his parent's love, is this candle ritual.

Parent (holding one candle): 'When you were born, you had the gift to give love and to get love. This gift is like a light; it makes you feel warm and happy.' (Then you light the candle representing the child.) 'At first you got used to your mum. She probably cuddled you and fed you. You felt close to her.' (And you put the child's lighted candle next to the unlit candle that represents the birth mother until it, too, lights.) 'And you lit a love light with each other.' Then you might go on, 'Your dad thought you were really special. He played with you when he came home from work. He helped with your bath. You felt close to him (putting the child's candle next to the candle for the father until it lights), and you lit a love light with him too.' Depending on the situation you might add, 'Your dad and mum stopped loving each other. Your dad went to live in a different house. But his love light for you still kept going, and your love light for him kept going too.'

You might go on, 'Your mum/dad is going to marry [new partner's name]. S/he will be living in your house and doing some of the things for you that your dad/mum used to do when your parents were still married. In time you may get used to having [new partner's name] help you with things. You may become close to him/her and s/he may become close to you.' (Light a new candle representing the step-parent). 'When that happens, there will be one more person for you to love and who loves you. The important thing for you to remember is that the light of love you feel for your dad/mum will not go out. Loving is not like soup that you dish out until it is all gone. You can love as many people as you get close to. But no one will make you blow out any of your candles. You do not have to take the love you feel for your dad/mum away to love [new partner's name].'

With whatever variation fits, you need to give the child *permission* to grow close to a new caregiver. This ritual is easily adapted to almost all circumstances where a child feels that s/he must extinguish her/his feelings for one important adult in order to please another. Because the candle was chosen for its symbolic connection with children's perception of love as light and warmth, it is important to close the ritual carefully, as in the following suggestion.

Parent: 'I can see, [child's name], that you understand about loving. I don't think you need the candles any more today to help you. This candle is not really your mother/father. S/he will not stop loving you if we put it out. Are you ready to help me blow it out?'

This needs to be repeated for each candle before it is extinguished.

Printed in the United Kingdom by
Lightning Source UK Ltd., Milton Keynes
137974UK00001BA/5/P